SO-BIX-036

TAMING THE STORM

LIBRARY OF WAYNE F. EMERY

19-HORN

TAMING
THE STORM

The Art of Synergy

TOM HORNSBY
AND LARRY WARKOCZESKI

4119-HORN

Copyright © 2002 by Visionworks, L.L.C.

Library of Congress Number:		2001127198
ISBN #:	Hardcover	1-4010-4347-X
	Softcover	1-4010-4346-1

All rights reserved. No part of this book may be reproduced or transmitted in any form or by any means, electronic or mechanical, including photocopying, recording, or by any information storage and retrieval system, without permission in writing from the copyright owner.

This is a work of fiction. Names, characters, places and incidents either are the product of the author's imagination or are used fictitiously, and any resemblance to any actual persons, living or dead, organizations, events, or locales is entirely coincidental.

This book was printed in the United States of America.

To order additional copies of this book, contact:
Xlibris Corporation
1-888-7-XLIBRIS
www.Xlibris.com
Orders@Xlibris.com

CONTENTS

In memory of

Rosa B. Jackson, my mother,
and
Natalie S. Stoughton, my mother-in-law.

You were peacemakers.

—

To my wife, Lynnis, and daughter, Melanie, and son,
Mark – thanks for your encouragement,
it is energizing.

—Tom Hornsby

4119-HORN

To my wife, Vicki, and son, Craig, and parents, Harold and Beverly, who have encouraged me to pursue my dreams.

— Larry Warkoczeski

Come to the edge
We can't, we are afraid

Come to the edge
We can't, we will fall

And they came to the edge

And he pushed them

And they flew

—**Appollinaire**

ACKNOWLEDGMENTS

Taming the Storm became a reality because of the encouragement and support of a number of people. Wherever we succeeded in this book, a special thanks is due to the many people who helped us along the way. Any of the shortcomings of this book can be directly attributed to our inability to translate our experiences onto paper.

Robert Coleman, a gifted artist, brought the characters of this book to life through his magical creations on paper.

The book concept was reinforced by the feedback we gained from our relationships with people from all walks of life. Kathryn Wilhoit, chief nursing officer, and Scott Williams, hospital administrator, for leading healthcare organizations, were especially helpful and avid practitioners. Our enthusiasm for the material and how it can affect people was renewed from our interac-

tions with Piyush Joshi, M.D., a widely respected trans-
plant surgeon. He truly applies synergy in his life.

Healthcare is not the only place where conflict grows
and festers. Conflict is alive within the hallowed cham-
bers of churches. Don Jeanes, President of Milligan Col-
lege, was concerned about the growing turnover of ministers in churches. He challenged us to help ministers,
leaders and members of churches constructively handle
conflict and channel their efforts. From this experience,
we fine-tuned our ideas for the book. We're thankful
for President Jeanes' advice, guidance and review of the
book draft. Reggie Weems, Ph.D., the senior minister
for a large congregation, was also instrumental in our
application of these ideas to the spiritual side of life.
His church staff was especially helpful as we applied the
synergy model to personal lives.

Using the synergy principles in Argentina and
Mexico, we found that conflict and synergy offer simi-
lar opportunities around the globe. Christian Alvarez
Vergara, Training Coordinator for Eastman Chemical
Mexicana, was kind enough to help us understand the
universal language of synergy.

We were greatly encouraged by John Vann, CEO of
Clinical Trial Management Services, Inc., and his strong
belief in and application of synergy and quality management in his organization. Nasry Rizk Ph.D. , formerly
with Lawter International Inc., taught us the value of
simplifying and shortening complicated learning inter-
ventions. Lowell Mays of Herndon, Mays & Skornicka
reminded us from his letters that synergy starts at home.
Kevin Kaiser, Kaiser Institute, underscored the impor-

tance of listening beyond the audible experience and using intuition.

Hopefully, we have helped people find a more meaningful way to deal with conflict, stress and anger. We're thankful for these opportunities to forge meaning and enlightenment out of conflict. We have attempted to use, in a meaningful way, the guiding principles our parents shared with us during the early years of our journey in life.

Tom Hornsby and Larry Warkoczeski

INTRODUCTION

Conflict is like carbon dioxide. Some carbon dioxide is necessary for life, too much can be harmful. Stress in society is increasing too fast, fueled largely by an inability to manage change. Change inherently results in conflict and an insatiable hunger for solutions. The number of conflict management books on bookstore shelves is hard, cold evidence of the growing prevalence.

Books on conflict share a consistent theme – manage the conflict. Some books emphasize listening skills. Many books suggest techniques to "get your way." Other books emphasize talking skills. Often, these books emphasize the conflict itself without focusing on solutions.

In a world where conflict abounds, these traditional views of conflict management are insufficient. Traditional views haven't decreased stress levels; in fact, they have increased stress levels. The solution is synergy. The key to synergy is understanding self and others using an effective communication process. Too often, individuals and groups fail to look beyond their own surroundings and to use other resources that can create synergy.

Stephen R. Covey, author of *The 7 Habits of Highly Effective People*, did a wonderful job convincing us that thinking win-win, listening and talking are important prerequisites to achieve synergy. *Taming the Storm: The Art of Synergy* goes one step further. This book provides a step-by-step process on how to synergize, both in the work setting and in personal lives to integrate facts, opinions, feelings and desires.

Unlike other conflict-oriented books, *Taming the Storm* is an entertaining and educational tale. The story makes it easy for individuals to learn and remember key points, unlike most conflict management books that require close and extended reading. *Taming the Storm* also provides "hooks" that individuals can later remember to increase their understanding and use of the model.

In this stressful and fast paced world, information needs to be provided and consumed within a short time period. Whether you're riding in a car, flying on an airplane or relaxing at home, *Taming the Storm* can be read in less than one hour.

In addition to the book's brevity, the synergy model that is used in *Taming the Storm* is simple, composed of four components. A vast number of conflict management books, on the other hand, offer five to seven steps. Frankly, it's difficult for individuals to remember and apply a model greater than four steps without the cumbersome use of note cards, job aids or other props.

By now, you may have noticed the phrase "art of synergy" is used in the title instead of the "science of synergy." Granted, achieving synergy requires the same basic steps in any complicated issue. However, the synergy process will vary from issue to issue because it's a dynamic effort or art affected by such things as culture and individual behaviors. Because of this, some steps may need to be repeated or certain steps may require greater emphasis than others. For beginners, the synergy process may require painstaking attention to each step while veterans may be able to move quickly from step to step.

In a world overcome with issues, individuals can view conflict as something to be sidestepped, controlled, or embraced. For individuals who wisely embrace conflict to improve decision-making, the keys to success are training and practice.

I encourage you to take the journey *Taming the Storm*.

T. O. Hobbes
March 1, 2002

CHAPTER 1

The Storm Before the Storm

Not even a black cat would risk crossing their path. Staring straight ahead, two managers, Frank and Mandy, marched down the sidewalk leading from the management conference center. Exchanging quizzical glances, two other managers, Kyle and Barbara, followed at a safe distance.

When the four managers reached the front of the General Store, Mandy abruptly faced Frank clenching her fists at her sides in uncharacteristic fashion. "I can't believe you'd say such a thing in that meeting."

"Believe it," Frank said as he shook his head.

Mandy raised her arms and shook her head. "You don't care at all about the people."

Normally low key and quiet, Frank was not about to back off. "More than you do."

"Oh, and that's why you sounded like a surgeon during an autopsy," Mandy said.

Frank inched closer. "It's a loser. You need to face it." Frank thought that Mandy didn't appreciate his comments; she didn't seem to care whether she understood his point of view or not. She seemed more concerned about protecting her pet project.

Mandy placed her hands on her hips and leaned forward. "Loser?"

"Throwing money down a hole," Frank said. "That's a loser."

Shaking her head, Mandy turned to walk away but suddenly lunged toward Frank. "You should know, Frank, your list of failures is as long as this road." Mandy had worked closely with Frank for several years and never before encountered this type of behavior from him. Without a doubt, she thought Frank must have a personal agenda and anyone associated with the e-commerce project was fair game. The fact he didn't care to hear her point of view was proof enough.

As Kyle sprang between them, Frank and Mandy stepped apart while cautiously watching each other. Frank's face was deep red while Mandy's jaw was tightening like a screw.

"Time out," Kyle said. "We're going to enjoy ourselves."

Turning around, Kyle opened the door to the General Store like a concierge. Without a word, Frank stomped into the General Store. Mandy passed through the doorway brushing against Kyle. "So, whose side are you on?"

"You're not going to draw me into this conflict," Kyle said. "And what makes you think there are different sides?"

Keeping a safe distance from Frank and Mandy, Barbara stopped long enough in the entrance to pat Kyle on the shoulder. "The first chance we get, we need to abandon ship and let them argue their day away, saving us from misery. I can't handle this."

The General Store was untouched by time except for electrical lights and a rotary-dial telephone. The air was filled with scents of spices and burning hickory wood. Kyle, Barbara and Mandy sat around a wood stove located in the middle of the room. While Mandy simmered, Kyle and Barbara gave a collective sigh of relief and began shucking peanuts that were overflowing from a barrel setting next to them. Hurriedly, Frank purchased four sodas while turning toward Mandy just long enough to scowl.

Frank had dropped the biggest bombshell at their management retreat when he asked whether their e-commerce division should be closed because of continued financial losses. For managers like Mandy who spent endless days creating the division, his words were as harsh as fingernails drawn across a blackboard. Uninvolved managers like Kyle and Barbara were caught in the middle of a cross-fire.

"I promise," Frank pronounced as he handed out the sodas, "I won't discuss the e-commerce issue any more this afternoon."

"We all agree," Kyle said. "It's time we mellow out."

Just as they relaxed in their seats, the entrance door slammed shut like a crocodile's jaws snapping at its prey. The conversation halted as their heads swiveled toward the door. There stood an Old Man wearing a discolored skippers cap frayed at the edges. As he walked toward the four, his pipe jumped toward them drawing attention to his bushy moustache. Without a word, he settled into a rocking chair next to Mandy and warmed his smooth outstretched hands by the fire. Mandy slowly slid to the opposite side of her chair. The others curiously watched the Old Man who seemed unaware of the surroundings. They could barely hear a strange tune coming from him. After several minutes, the four resumed a hushed conversation like a church congregation prior to Sunday services. All the while, the Old Man rocked to and fro, staring into the fire. As time passed, Mandy and Barbara chatted incessantly stopping only long enough to drink their sodas.

While Kyle recited the General Store's history from memory, Frank leaned toward Mandy and Barbara straining to catch a few words. Several times, Frank caught himself tipping sideways in his seat.

When Mandy and Barbara mentioned the morning retreat session, Frank dove headway into the conversation.

"Mandy," Frank said, "I don't appreciate being called a failure." Mandy's words continued to eat away at Frank. It was obvious to him that she didn't want to hear about his concerns.

Barbara shook her head while she covered her face with both hands. Mandy leaped to her feet and turned toward Frank like a lazy susan spinning out of control.

"You're like a snail, Frank," Mandy said. "You come out of your shell once in a while. And, this time you slimed an entire project." She was a bit surprised by her own words.

Kyle and Barbara stared wide-eyed in disbelief toward Mandy; Frank leaped to his feet.

"Steady as she goes," the Old Man said. Frank stumbled back into his chair. Mandy's feet seemed glued to the floor as she stood staring at the Old Man. Both Kyle and Barbara sat straight in their seats. The only sound in the room was the Old Man's heavy breathing.

"I saw you in front of the store jabbering at each other," the Old Man declared. "But, no one is going to make a sound in here. Instead, I'm going to share a story about taming the storm."

Startled by the Old Man, no one dared move except to slowly nod in agreement. The Old Man sat back in his rocking chair. He started talking in a deep, haunting voice while pointing his pipe toward the exposed rafters above their heads.

CHAPTER 2

The Storm

Once, just off the Carolina coast, there was a boat drifting in the ocean with three fishermen, John, Tom and Simon. They were weekend fishermen using the sea as a playground.

As they brought in their catch, John and Simon were locked in a duel seeing who could land the biggest fish. Simon tested John's patience by grabbing his skipper's hat and parading around the deck. John appeared slightly annoyed as he focused on his fishing line trailing in the water. Meanwhile, Tom fumbled with the bait readjusting his feet as they shifted on the slippery deck. The old, wooden fishing trawler with a motor trailing in the waters abruptly rocked from side to side. Unlike his shipmates, Tom was barely able to keep from losing his breakfast.

Past midday, clouds suddenly rolled in as harsh flashes of lightning and thunderous booms filled the air. The waves began to leap inside the boat as the fishermen scurried to reel in their lines. The faster they worked the more the wind pushed the boat farther out to sea.

Suddenly, the ocean began to heave, foaming with giant waves. As the boat swung downward in the air, her huge motor ripped loose from the aft spinning out of control. John screamed as the propeller blade sliced his right thigh. As he writhed in pain, the motor continued forward and crashed into the instrument panel before falling into the gray, swirling waters. Their cooler of food and water and the sea-to-shore radio quickly followed the motor into the ocean.

The fishermen's terror was louder than their cries for help. The rain turned day into night leaving each of the fishermen to grope in darkness for a part of the boat to grasp. With each violent wave, the fishermen slid around in the boat the same as the fish they caught earlier in the day. The boat moaned and creaked as the three ricocheted off the sides of the boat. As the boat abruptly dropped from the top of a wave, Tom slammed sideways into the hull. Despite the noise from the storm, he could hear a cracking sound similar to a tree splitting in two.

The storm subsided just as quickly as it began, leaving dark clouds and no trace of the sun. The large waves were replaced with two-feet whitecaps playing against the side of the boat. The boat was afloat but it barely resembled its previous outline. The aft of the boat was low in the water; the sea eased through the ragged edges where the motor used to be. The fishermen's hair and clothing were matted in crazy quilt fashion. Blood oozed from a gash in John's right leg. John quickly covered the wound with a strip of clothing torn from the bottom of his shirt; he tied a tourniquet at the top of his leg. Simon was more fortunate as he stumbled about the deck nursing only bumps and bruises and a slight cut on his forehead.

"Where are we?" Tom cried as he cradled his right arm. The injured arm was swollen and blue.

John was no stranger to these waters but the storm had twisted the ocean in every direction. "I don't know," he said in a barely audible voice.

"We can't stay out here for long," Simon said.

"Steady as she goes," John said. "That's important."

"We can't stay afloat more than a few hours." Simon was already surveying the boat.

The fishermen rummaged around the boat for anything that might help them paddle the boat. John found a lone board from the instrument panel and his hat wedged between the sides of the boat. He quickly pried the board loose while he stuffed his hat back into his pocket. Dropping the board into the water, John began paddling with growing confidence.

Tom continued to nurse his swollen arm while John and Simon took turns paddling the boat. As minutes turned into hours, there was still no sign of shore. Several times, John changed course as he searched for any sign of land.

Soon confidence gave way to desperation, as they feared the worst. John and Simon tussled with the board as Tom tried to wedge between them. Standing a good half-foot shorter and forty pounds lighter than either of the other two men, Tom was easily pushed aside as he screamed for the two to listen to him. Being the most vocal and persistent, Simon changed their course confident that the shoreline was in the opposite direction.

After another hour, there were still no signs of life. The boat seemed to rest deeper in the water. Nerves frayed as John and Simon exchanged cutting remarks, while blaming each other for their plight. All the while, Tom struggled to no avail to quiet the storm on board.

Just as they began to change direction for a fifth time, they saw a distant object bobbing among the waves. At first, it looked like a buoy floundering in the ocean. As the object came closer, they could see it was an owl standing on a broken board. In minutes, the owl came to rest against their boat. Then, it leisurely jumped into the boat and sat observing the fishermen. After several minutes, John and Simon forgot about the owl and resumed their bickering.

"If you'd just give me the paddle for more than one minute, we'd be back on shore," John protested as he pried the board from Simon's hands.

"You're the mighty sailor," Simon panted as he struggled to regain the board. "We're lost without power or food because of you." Simon finally wrested the board from John's grasp. "We're going home even if I have to pull this boat with my teeth while I do the backstroke."

"That would be a very interesting picture, indeed."

All three stopped and looked toward the owl.

"Did you say something, Tom?" John asked.

"Not me," Tom answered as he grimaced in pain.

"Now you're really losing it," Simon said. "You think a stupid bird can talk."

"Precisely," the owl said as he walked toward the center of the boat. "At this rate, you'll never find shore. You're going in circles."

"And – And you think you know better?" John asked.

The owl turned to face John. "With all due respect— yes I do."

"I'll be," Simon said. "The bird talks."

"Please, please, please. I'm an owl. And that is a *fact*. A talking owl. And that is also a *fact*."

John was growing more anxious by the moment. "Can you find shore?"

"Why, no. I assure you that you can do that," the owl pronounced as he pointed his wing toward them. "I'll help you solve that issue."

Both John and Simon nervously laughed and ridiculed the owl. Who would listen to a bird especially when they were stuck in the middle of the ocean? Tom, on the other hand, walked over to the owl, sat down, and patiently waited for the catcalls from John and Simon to subside.

As John and Simon resumed their argument, Tom whispered to the owl. "I've never been so scared in all my life. I don't know if I'll ever see my wife and kids again. We're—we're going nowhere, aren't we?"

"Fear is a grim reminder of the storm. You are to be commended for admitting your fear," the owl said as he carefully patted Tom on his back. "You're correct, though. You're going nowhere. I think you've found the limits to conflict and realize it can send you in circles. One word, my friend, synergy."

"Synergy?" At first, Tom thought the owl might offer hope. But, now, Tom was beginning to wonder.

"You're focusing on the conflict," the owl said. "In-

stead, you need to focus on understanding each other)
and the solution. Synergy."

"That doesn't make any sense," Tom said.

"Synergy is all of us. One plus three is five," the owl
said. "Synergy is finding resolution. You do this by in-
tertwining each of your understandings of the situation
and solutions. Together, you can find ways to an end
that you wouldn't find alone."

"But how?" Tom was still not convinced.

"It's about synergy leadership, not conflict management," the owl said as he scratched words into the hull
of the boat. "You humans haven't figured that out, have
you? You must manage the solution, not the conflict. ⟨
Instead of trying to get the fishermen to stop arguing,
you need to encourage them to share their impressions.
Otherwise, you're wasting valuable energy and time."

As Tom looked toward John and Simon who were
arguing over the paddle, he began to realize what the
owl was saying. They had spent all of their energy arguing who was right and who was wrong. Without any hesitation, Tom asked the owl to help them.

The owl immediately offered four key steps to reach
synergy: Identify Issue, Understand You, Understand Me, ∠
and Solution(s). Tom quickly agreed with the owl that
the issue was quite clear. They needed to find safety from
the harsh ocean.

"I'm sure you realize," said the owl, "the issues will
look somewhat different as you understand everyone's
view of the crisis. You need to clearly define the Issue,
identify who is involved and determine if the issue is
important enough to do something about it." Even
though Tom nodded his head, the owl didn't appear convinced that Tom appreciated what he said.

With a 180° twist of his head, the owl slowly began asking several questions. Did Tom try listening to John and Simon or did he do as the others? Was Tom able to understand why John and Simon acted the way they did? What solutions might John and Simon offer? Tom knew the owl was right. Instead of trying to listen to John and Simon, Tom only screamed at them. He tried to convince them to listen to him. No one in the boat was listening to understand. Instead, words were being used like a ping-pong ball bouncing from one person to another.

"Humans have a very consistent pattern, if I might say so," the owl said. "Humans like to be understood, first. Then, and only then, they will try to understand others. The problem is – not everyone can be understood first. That's one of the secrets to success. First, listen. I like to refer to it as 'I Understand You.' It's a wonderful phrase because it's easy to remember and is very clear."

"It sounds simple," Tom said. "Too simple. Shouldn't it be more complex?"

"That's the beauty of it." The owl continued to scratch a number of words into the side of the boat. "It doesn't need to be complicated because humans are not that complex when it comes to conflict." The owl explained the power of "I Understand You" noting that people are not used to others using the tool. When they hear someone wanting to understand them, they're usually ready to cooperate because they want to be understood.

"One word of warning. John and Simon will not open up and share their feelings and thoughts unless they're convinced that Tom really cares about them personally," the owl said as he finished his writing on the hull. "That only happens when they're satisfied Tom will truly listen and use their input." As the owl stepped to the side, he pointed to the phrase "Understand You" that he had etched into the side of the boat.

All the while, the boat drifted aimlessly about the ocean. The sky seemed to crack as sporadic lightning bolts shot through the distant, dark sky.

4119-HORN

CHAPTER 3

In Search of the Calm

The three fishermen were as hungry as they were tired. It had been hours since their last meal. John's leg was no longer bleeding, however, he hobbled more noticeably across the deck. Tom's arm was a darker blue and more swollen than before.

"We've got to find something to eat." John scoured the deck again to see if any food had fallen out before the cooler went overboard. "Or, we'll never have enough strength to paddle to shore."

Simon reminded John that all of their food was washed overboard because they were unprepared for the storm. "Maybe, you might want to try the owl. I've never tasted owl before."

"I've never tasted owl, either," the owl added without hesitation. "But, I don't believe you need to reach that point. You have plenty of crackers in your pockets. They may be a bit broken from being tossed around, but they should do."

All three reached deep into their soggy pockets. One

by one they pulled out packages of crackers. They tore them open and began to down the pieces like water.

"How did you know that?" Tom was amazed.

"Before you were fishing, you placed the crackers in your pockets to snack on while you watched your fishing poles. I might suggest that you ration those crackers. You don't know how long you may be here. It all depends on how long it takes for you to achieve synergy."

The owl nudged Tom with his wing. He whispered the words "I Understand You."

Tom was hesitant. He wasn't comfortable in this role. In his business, he was more comfortable dealing with numbers than people. But, he knew the group wouldn't make any progress unless they changed their approach to the problem. The owl winked at Tom and pointed to the phrase "Understand You" etched into the hull.

Reluctantly, Tom interrupted their dinner armed with the wisdom of the owl. "I—I've been thinking. I've known both of you longer than anyone else in my life, including my wife. We've gone through a lot together."

"More than we realize," John added as he carefully ate the remaining crumbs from the wrapper.

"We stood by each other during John's wife's battle with cancer," Tom said. "And Simon, you helped me out when no one else believed me and my partners could make our accounting practice go."

"You'd do the same." Simon nodded his head.

"I'm determined—we're all going to get out of here alive. Besides, I can't lose two of my clients. My accounting partners would never forgive me."

"Good, very good," the owl whispered. "Honest and from the heart with a little levity thrown in for good measure." He nudged Tom encouraging him to proceed.

Despite feeling clumsy, Tom continued focusing on

the words "Pay Attention" etched below the phrase "Understand You". He admitted to John and Simon that he knew nothing about the ocean. It was his first time out and hopefully not his last. But he did know that unless they created a plan of action, they were going to be floating around the ocean until the boat sank. Tom realized that they had been doing a lot of talking. But he hadn't paid much attention to what they said. He asked them what they needed to do to get out of this predicament.

Without hesitation, Simon responded. "We need to get out of this boat. It's going to sink. Waves are rushing into the aft. Another storm and we're through. And, we can thank John for that."

"Maybe, I need to remind you." John struggled to his feet and pointed at Simon. "You didn't want to wait this morning. Instead of checking the weather, we left port. I knew better than to depend on last night's report."

"What do we need to do to get out of this predicament?" Tom asked. The owl had warned him that he would need to be persistent to gain their best thinking. Tom knew that Simon was going to be the most difficult person to deal with during the process because he was very competitive.

For the first time following the storm, John spoke with confidence. "We need to find shore. Instead of jabbering, we need a focus. We're floundering without a focus. Once we determine where shore is located, we can begin to make progress." As he ended his comments, John paused and added, "I feel like I let the group down. I don't think I've ever done that before in my life. I used to think I was a pretty good skipper but now I'm angry with myself and I'm embarrassed. I've let you down. I've let myself down."

For a few minutes, the only sound was the lapping of the waves against the side of the boat. Tom knew John's ending comments were difficult to share because John was especially proud of his boating skills. The silence was surprising to Tom as he expected Simon to use the opportunity to blame John again for their plight.

The owl, once again, nudged Tom pointing to the words he had scratched into the wooden hull – "Sum Up."

"I appreciate all of your comments," Tom said. "John, I appreciate your courage for sharing your feelings. I know I feel angry and embarrassed. You're not alone." Tom paused as he nodded toward John. "Okay. Let's sum up your points. We're lost; the boat is badly damaged and may sink. We have little or no food and water and we need to find shore."

The others nodded their heads. The owl cleared his throat and pointed to the cryptic words scratched into the wood – "Ask Questions." Nodding his head, Tom began asking questions about how long they could last in the boat. How long could they survive with little or no food and water? Simon and John were intently listening to his questions. Is there a way to determine the direction of the shoreline? Was anyone likely to start looking for them at this point in time?

John was confident the boat would last through the night because it wasn't taking on more water. They could go without food and water for a couple of days if they conserved their energy. As for a rescue team, Simon knew that a team would not look for them until they failed to return to shore that evening. The likelihood of seeing another boat on the water was slim because most boats would have returned to shore.

As John nodded his head, he said they could normally identify the direction of the shoreline by the sun.

Without the sun to guide them, the shoreline would be difficult to find because of the cloud cover. They could, however, determine the direction of the tide if they were close enough to shore. It should be late enough in the afternoon for the incoming tide to be starting.

"Excellent, excellent!" the owl expounded.

"What has gotten into your friend, Tom?" John asked.

"I think you've made great progress." The owl patted each fisherman on the back with his wing. "You need to celebrate with one more package of crackers. Down the proverbial hatch."

As John and Simon each gleefully swallowed the remnants of another pack of crackers, they failed to hear a distant rumbling noise. Several lightning bolts pierced the sky as the boat jostled to and fro. The wind picked up as the waves slapped the side of the boat. Tom warned the owl that more water was surely seeping into the boat. Dismayed, Tom felt their progress had come too late to save them.

CHAPTER 4

The Clearing

As the thunder grew louder, the owl grew more focused on his conversation with Tom. John and Simon were still excited about their progress even to the point of daydreaming out loud about the first thing they would do when they reached shore.

"We may have made too little progress too late," Tom said as he pointed toward the massive black cloud.

"It isn't always the black cloud that you need to be most concerned about," the owl said. He went on to explain that they needed to focus on things they could do something about. They needed to be concerned about the boat where they could have the greatest impact. As the unannounced leader of the group, Tom was encouraged to sort out his thoughts and share them with his shipmates.

Tom felt overwhelmed. He had just bared his soul to his longtime friends and now the owl expected him to go one step farther.

"I don't know anything about the ocean," Tom exclaimed. "They'll just laugh at me if they haven't already."

"How will they know what you think? You now understand them. They need to understand your point of view," the owl said. "Only then, can the group achieve synergy, my friend. The other alternative is we can sit and watch the black cloud and let it determine our fate."

Tom stared toward the black cloud that was sweeping toward them. "For more than ten years, I've flown a hot air balloon never expecting a storm would get the best of me. Even when I ran into a hailstorm that shredded my balloon, I was able to land safe on my feet. The first time on the ocean and my luck may run out."

"It isn't about luck," the owl said. "It's about moving forward and synergy. Frankly, I wouldn't allow a temporary storm to get me down or in my way. This is nothing more than the hailstorm that shredded your balloon. It's your choice whether you return safely to your wife and children."

Those final words were enough to prod Tom. With encouragement from Tom, the owl explored the third part of the model, "Understand Me," that was etched into the side of the boat. For success, Tom would need to consider from his point of view the three parts that the owl had etched into the hull.

Before they continued, the owl offered some insight to Tom. "Opinions cloud facts like the overcast days cover up the sun. It's important to distinguish between facts and opinions. Too often, we tend to look at only the facts. Conflict is only seen as a duel between the facts."

"That's not so difficult," Tom replied. As Tom carefully sorted out the facts from the opinions, the owl offered suggestions. Several times, Tom struggled to determine the difference between facts and opinions. Finally, Tom was now prepared to share his thoughts with his shipmates.

"You see," the owl said, "it isn't quite as easy as you thought. The facts aren't always clear."

"So, I just need to worry about facts and opinions?" Tom asked.

"Not quite. What about feelings and desires?" The owl seemed to be stroking his whiskers. "Feelings and desires can be just as important. But, they are difficult to dredge up because you must take a chance. With human beings, feelings and desires are a source of energy. John has certainly shared his feelings. Remember, think it through means all four pieces of information – feelings, desires, opinions and facts."

"I guess I tend to think of my opinions as facts. And, you're right, I haven't shared my feelings."

"Sharing your feelings is not showing a weakness, it's showing your strength of heart," the owl said.

As Tom steadied his feet, he approached the others to sum up his point of view. He was more nervous than he had been when he earlier shared his fears with the owl. Tom thanked the owl for helping them work on the solution. Taking a deep breath, Tom shared his perceptions with the group.

"This may sound crazy, but I just realized that we're

not really lost," Tom said. "You see, we know we're in the ocean."

"That's what you're thinking?" Simon snickered.

"Well, that and more. We can't be too far out from the shore. And, despite the damage the boat is still floating."

"It may be floating now," Simon said, "but-"

"In fact, the boat may be our solution after all," Tom declared. He continued underscoring the importance of the boat. The boat would buy them time to focus their efforts. The boat might even float to shore. He admitted that food and water could become a problem if they were unable to find shore by nightfall.

As he concluded, Tom offered the owl's comments on the importance of both opinions and facts. "Everyone is tired. Our feelings are mostly about anger. We're angry at each other. And John is taking too much of the blame. We all share responsibility for our situation. We need to focus our energy on finding the solution."

Except for the approaching thunder, there was silence. As they all looked nervously at each other, Simon slowly stepped forward and offered his outstretched hand to John. "I think Tom is talking about me. I'm sore and taking it out on you. Actually, I'm as mad at myself as I am you. Yes, I pushed you into leaving port before we should have."

"You don't need to say another word." John grasped Simon's hand with both of his hands.

As John and Simon patted each other on the back, Tom asked if they had any questions for him.

After a few moments, Simon asked why Tom thought the boat would stay afloat. Tom admitted, "It's a gut feeling."

"Your gut may be right," John said. "The water line

in the boat hasn't risen in several hours and we're no deeper in the water than before."

As Simon sat down, John asked Tom why he thought the shoreline must be nearby. On this point, Tom offered he was more confident because they had not journeyed out too far from shore and the storm did not last a long time. It was unlikely they could have drifted very far.

"And we should realize from my earlier comments," the owl added, "that whatever distance you covered with your paddling was merely in a circle."

"So, you think we may be closer to shore than some of us thought?" Looking out over the water, John squinted as he slowly nodded his head. "You may be right."

"What do we do now?" Tom asked the owl.

The owl walked into the middle of the group and winked at Tom. "You now know what each of you think. It's time to work on the solution. It's closer than you realize."

"But, where do we start?" they asked in unison.

"The pieces of the puzzle are on the table. Some pieces are facts. Others are feelings. While others are opinions. Even your desires are on the table," the owl said. "I'd suggest that you build from the pieces of information you can agree upon."

"I think we agreed that the boat was stable for a period of time," Tom recounted. "We also agreed that we were angry at each other and it may keep us from focusing on our solution. It seems we all had the same desire to reach shore. If we're going to reach shore by nightfall though, we can't depend on others to find us. I'm not as sure on this point, but I think we agreed that we may not be that far from shore."

The three fishermen discussed these points reaching agreement except on the first point.

Simon told the group that he wasn't comfortable the boat would survive another storm. Simon asked John for his opinion.

Admitting the storm had severely damaged the boat, John recognized that another storm could be devastating. Therefore, the boat could put them at risk the longer they searched for shore or awaited rescue.

"Quickly, now," the owl advised, "let's identify the solutions."

"I tend to see a number of possible solutions to this situation. But, only a couple of them seem to make sense to me," Simon said. "We could do nothing and wait for help, determine the direction of the tide and paddle toward shore, or piece together a flag from clothing in anticipation of rescue the following day."

"You've done a splendid job," the owl said as he patted Simon on the shoulder. "My suggestion is that you now take these three solutions and decide which one is best. If you have other solutions, add them to the list."

"How do we sort through them after we get down to the two or three best solutions?" John asked. "Each person is bound to think his idea is better than someone else's idea." The other two fishermen nodded their heads in agreement.

"Good observation," the owl said. "The key is to evaluate the impact of each option on each person affected. In other words, people need to think beyond self. I like to use pluses and minuses to evaluate the impact."

"I think I followed you," John said, "until you got to the pluses and minuses."

"For each solution," the owl said, "ask yourself if it is good for you. If it is, it is a plus. Then, ask if the solution is good for the others in your group. If it is, it is a plus."

"And, what if it isn't a plus?" Simon asked.

"It's a minus," the owl said. "Try to think of the plus as worth one point and a minus is worth a negative one point. Add these up and you will identify the stronger solutions. So, if it is good for me and not good for you, it has a zero value."

The three began to sort out the possible solutions. Each of them offered what they believed were the best solutions based on all of the information. Since they agreed it was important to boil down to two or three solutions, they identified where they agreed upon feelings, desires, opinions and facts and evaluated the impact. As they looked at the results, they agreed upon two solutions: (1) they could determine the tide and pursue the shoreline or (2) create a flag from clothing in anticipation of a rescue mission the next day.

They felt good about the progress they made. This was the first time they cooperated to find a solution to their conflict. The owl encouraged them to take one more step and see if they could agree upon the best solution.

Adding the pluses and minuses, the fishermen agreed that the best solution was to identify the tide and locate the shoreline. They agreed that they would create a flag from clothing if they were unable to discover the shoreline before darkness prevailed.

John took a piece of shattered wood and dropped it into the water. This would help them determine the direction of the tide. They all watched as the piece of wood drifted to their right.

"If we're correct, we need to paddle in that direction," John observed. "If not, we could be running out to sea."

"What if the owl flew overhead to see if he could spot shore?" Tom asked. "With his keen eyesight, that should give us better odds. I think we'd all feel more comfortable."

The owl vigorously flapped his wings as he stood in place. "Superb. Definitely an example of synergy. Despite your lack of expertise on the high seas, you recognized that the group hadn't used all of the resources available to solve the issues."

John and Simon agreed and encouraged the owl to spread his wings.

"Gentlemen, let's put this plan into action. We're now synergy mates." With one giant leap, the owl thrust into the sky circling the boat several times as he rose higher. Swooping over the boat one last time, the owl pointed his wing to the right in the same direction as the drifting wood.

With a sudden turn, he headed in the opposite direction toward the open sea. Simon and John scurried sharing the paddling chores.

Tom turned and watched the owl disappear. "You never told us your name." The owl continued flying. As Tom looked down, he saw a name scratched into the hull. Hobbes. "*Goodbye, Hobbes,*" Tom said to himself. "*And thank you for your gift.*"

With the thrust of the tide and the hopes of the three remaining synergy mates, the boat ended up waddling onto the beach just as darkness fell and lightning broke the sky. As they stumbled out of the boat onto shore, the synergy mates could see the outline of a house nestled between two sand dunes located straight ahead. Tom continued to cradle his injured arm but he no longer felt the pain because of his elation. Not far behind, John hobbled through the sand and stopped next to Tom while Simon dropped to his knees and scooped up the sand as he laughed.

"I think you deserve this," John said as he placed the skippers cap into Tom's hand.

"I don't deserve this." Tom knew the hat was important to John because he always had a treasured place for the cap on his mantle in his home. It was the hat John's father had worn on his last ocean voyage.

"You helped us tame the storm. Our storm." John patted Tom on the nape of his neck. "You never gave up, despite all our comments. Because of that, we're here on dry land. Thank you. Skipper."

After several failed attempts to return the cap, Tom unfolded it and placed it on his head. He felt lightheaded like he had when he captained his first hot air balloon flight – an exhilaration he thought he would never experience twice. It seemed as though the world was rotating around that exact spot on the beach. For a brief moment, Tom thought he could hear Hobbes flapping his wings in celebration.

CHAPTER 5

Understanding the Storm

The Old Man slowly rose from the rocking chair. "I've left you a tale to help tame your own storm. Without synergy, conflict can be destructive. It's your choice. You can manage conflict all day and still have no synergy. Manage synergy and you too will find the shore." The Old Man placed the pipe in his mouth and turned toward the door.

As the Old Man trudged toward the door, Mandy raised her hand in the air and swung it back and forth. "Your name? We never caught your name."

"You can call me, Tom. Fair weather to all of you," the Old Man said as he pushed open the door and disappeared outside.

"He's Tom from the story," Barbara gasped.

"But, what does the storm have to do with us?" Frank said as he scratched his head.

"We're in a storm, too. Tom was talking about us," Barbara said. "Before we walked in here, I thought we were in a tornado over this e-commerce thing. I'll be honest. I felt very uncomfortable and I wanted out."

"You're not the only one," Kyle added. "I just tried to ignore the conflict. I didn't help matters much."

"And, none of us tried to work on a solution," Frank said as he realized he failed to go beyond his own concerns. Instead of trying to understand others, Frank thought he had been too busy dealing with his own emotions. During the entire conflict, he also failed to share the reasons for his comments and his over-riding fear that the company would be devastated by the continued losses in the e-commerce division.

"That's right," Mandy added. "We were too busy attacking each other. I was guilty of focusing on the conflict. I just got angrier and angrier. I should've listened and asked you, Frank, why you said what you did at the retreat." As she shook her head, Mandy thought about how she leaped to conclusions about Frank's motives without understanding his percep-tions.

"You're not alone, Mandy. I should have been listening to you. Then, I would've shared more of my thoughts about why I questioned the e-commerce di-vision," Frank said. "Instead, I just let my feelings get the best of me. Man, the owl was right. Feelings and desires are important to people. They definitely in-fluence the way we look at issues. I learned that lesson the hard way."

"How about we work on our synergy?" Barbara asked.

"I'd love it," Mandy said as she stood extending her hand to Frank. "And this time, we're going to do it right."

"Synergy it is," Frank said as he shook Mandy's hand.

"This is as good a place as any to find synergy,"

Kyle added. "Better than a leaky boat in the middle of an ocean."

The discussion around the stove in the General Store was as lively as ever. They failed to notice the Old Man staring through the front window of the store. He took the pipe out of his mouth just long enough to smile. Then, he turned and disappeared down the street.

CHAPTER 6

How to Tame a Storm

A storm is a tidal wave of energy. Mankind has failed to harness the energy of storms such as thunderstorms or hurricanes, allowing them to dissipate, slip away or destroy everything in their paths. Similar to a weather storm, oftentimes people have storms and fail to harness the energy generated by these conflicts. The Old Man in the General Store offered Mandy, Frank, Barbara and Kyle wisdom about how to channel the energy from a storm. He referred to it as "taming the storm."

The Old Man's advice is a new way to think about conflict. By understanding the feelings, desires, opinions and facts of all individuals involved in a conflict, it is desirable and possible for individuals to harness their mental and emotional energy to reach a solution that is better than what any one individual would normally develop. This approach is about using energy created from conflict to reach unbounded levels and occasionally miraculous solutions. The Old Man learned from his fishing experience that proper channeling of conflict leads to synergy and a better solution supported by those affected by the issue.

As conflicts seem to grow faster than solutions in our society, people thirst for agreement. They are tired of increased stress created from the growing number of conflicts in their lives. Instead of being in disagreement, they want to find harmony through a solution that is good for all concerned. True harmony or synergy is the result of constructively handling conflict. The Old Man provided such a process. However, the Old Man was not talking about compromise.

Compromise is where each person gives up something to relieve tension. Ultimately, each individual leaves the agreement thinking that they have been deprived in order to gain only a part of what they desired. Over time, the solution is likely to fall apart as disgruntled individuals revisit what they gave up and what they received from the compromise. Frequently, compromise is a part time solution waiting for another storm. This is a tool commonly used by politicians.

Instead, the Old Man was talking about integration. The term, integration, was best defined by Mary Parker Follett in the 1920s. An example Ms. Follett used was the situation where two individuals could not agree whether a window in a room should remain opened or closed. The solution was to open a window in the next room allowing fresh air to reach the room and addressing concerns of the other individual who wanted to avoid a direct chilling breeze. Each individual felt they had reached a solution without depriving themselves of something in order to reach closure. They were in agreement, not compromise.

The Old Man also emphasized the importance of surfacing all points of view in order to create synergy. Not only should individuals share differences, they must share points of agreement. Most importantly, the Old Man underscored the sharing of all the key pieces of information including feelings, desires, opinions and facts. In other words, resolving conflict is not a debate just on the facts. This only creates greater friction and widens the gap among individuals. A focus only on facts fails to recognize the powerful impact of desires, feelings and opinions upon individuals.

For a few more minutes, join us, once again, in the boat as we explore more about the Synergy Model.

So, What Is The Synergy Model?

The owl, Hobbes scratched into the boat's hull a simple but dynamic tool – the Synergy Model. The purpose of the model was to provide an easy to understand approach to resolve conflict. The best way to understand the Synergy Model is to dissect it step by step.

Synergy Model

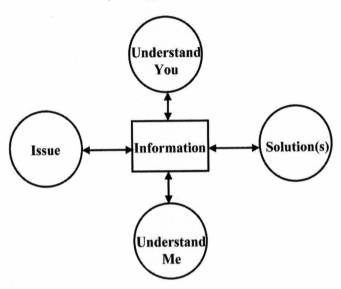

The Synergy Model consists of four major components each displayed in a circle. Thanks to Hobbes, it's easy to remember the four components. These are Issue, Understand You, Understand Me and Solution(s).

You might wonder why the word "Information" is located in a box in the middle of the model. From Issue, Understand You, Understand Me and Solution(s), individuals give and receive Information. The four components are interdependent as reflected by arrows pointing to and from each component. Information includes facts, feelings, opinions and desires associated with any issue. Obtaining and clarifying Information is foundational for two individuals or a group in conflict to determine the best solution(s). This is why Information is shown at the center of the model. In other words, the quality of the Solution(s) is directly related to the quality of the Information shared and understood.

Identifying the issue is the starting point. Frequently, individuals waste time because the Issue is not accurately stated or clearly understood. It is possible to develop a great solution for the wrong Issue. The important point is to spend the necessary time to clarify the Issue. Effectiveness here, not efficiency, will save time. As synergy is pursued, the Issue is crystallized throughout the process. From Information provided by others, the Issue will likely start to look different than originally perceived because others have different vantage points or paradigms. Therefore, it is important to gain an accurate understanding of the Issue as early as possible.

Understand You is a very important component because it underscores how critical it is to first listen empathetically to others. As Hobbes stated in the tale, Tom could not gain the other fishermen's trust to share their information unless they knew that Tom cared about them personally. This would require listening on Tom's part. The other fishermen must be convinced they are understood from their point of view. The other fishermen must also be convinced that Tom is willing to be influenced too. There is a difference between listening and waiting to be heard. Just as Tom realized, listening comes first. Synergy cannot be gained until the facts, feelings, opinions and desires of other individuals are clearly understood. Frequently, best solutions come from outsiders or people not as close to the issue.

With a clear understanding of others, it is just as important to Understand Me. Both listening and talking are essential in good communication. Tom in our tale wanted to avoid this part of the model because he was hesitant to speak out on a subject where he was less knowledgeable than John and Simon. However, Tom discovered that synergy wasn't possible until everyone understood each other. It also appears that Tom learned to appreciate the importance of both technical skills and good process skills to create synergy. In the end, Tom found it was important for him to share his facts, feelings, opinions and desires.

With Information in hand, the parties to the conflict can work together to develop Solution(s). This may take some discussion and several attempts to reach agreement upon the major elements associated with the Issue. Tom, John and Simon used a good decision process of adding up the pluses and minuses for each possible solution. There is great temptation to develop a solution only using the Information according to Understand Me. In other words, my point of view becomes the Information or my paradigm is the only paradigm. Resist that temptation! It is impossible to reach synergy – a higher level of solutions – without Information gained from Understand You. All of us are smarter than one individual if we are skilled in valuing diverse viewpoints.

With Information in hand, a number of potential solutions can be generated. However, Solution(s) needs to be based on agreed upon Information. Anything less is likely to lead to failure or discontent. If the Information is not clearly understood and agreed upon, the Solution(s) will be as hazy as the shore that John wrestled to identify. Also individuals involved in the conflict will not buy into the solution and embrace it (i.e., lack of ownership). The intent of the Synergy Model is to strive for total agreement and settle for no less than consensus. Total agreement means that the parties agree with the decision and will support it. On the other hand, consensus means that all individuals will support the decision even if they don't fully agree. Obviously, total agreement is the preferred approach. Tom, John and Simon used a good process to agree upon the solution, thanks to Hobbes. Once the three agreed upon the Information and the Solution(s), they strongly implemented and supported the direction taken. Before they reached that point, they were constantly changing direction and bickering and coming closer to death.

Okay, What Is The Synergy Process?

Once the Synergy Model is understood, it is important to master the Synergy Process. Unfortunately, Hobbes did not leave a diagram of the Synergy Process before he flew off into the distance. Therefore, the Synergy Process will be defined and explained.

Similar to the Synergy Model, the Synergy Process uses the same four major components or sub-processes: Issue, Understand You, Understand Me and Solution(s). We have included a detailed flow diagram for your review that traces each step of the process.

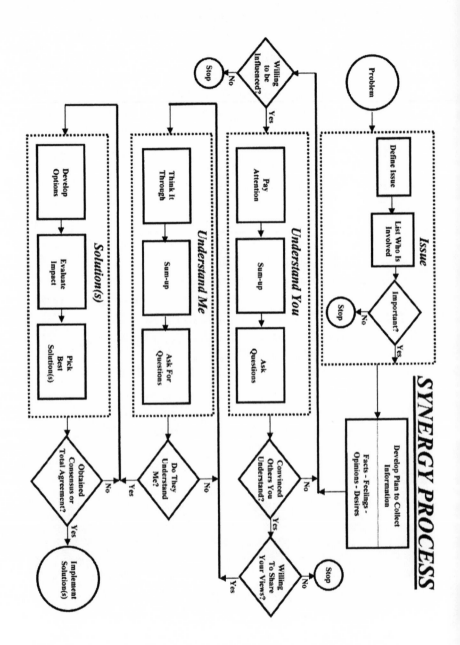

Issue

When sitting in the middle of the ocean in a damaged boat, no power, no electronic communication and little food and water, it's rather easy to define the issue. Find land. Oftentimes in our lives, it is not easy to identify the issue. Sometimes, an issue that is identified is really an outcome of the real problem. For example, an organization lost hundreds of thousands of dollars from scrap material. The leadership initially defined the issue as uncaring employees. Later, they redefined the issue. The issue was an apparent faulty process used to cut and trim parts. Employees were only using the low quality process forced on them.

Other times, a change in some of the "facts" may provide a much different situation. What if *Taming the Storm* dealt with a damaged boat in the middle of a harbor? The issue would no longer be focused on "find land." Instead, the problem would be focused on communication with people in other boats to gain help. Part of the problem in identifying an issue is the perception or vantage point of individuals. Because individuals see only part of the picture or a picture of reality from a certain perspective, it may be a challenge to define the issue. The definition of the issue usually becomes clearer as more information is shared.

It is important to get started. Therefore, an individual or group should define the issue. It is reasonable to expect that the definition of the issue may change as more information is shared and a better understanding is gained. This is acceptable and normal when in pursuit of synergy.

The definition of the issue will affect individuals who are included in the Synergy Process. Identify who is involved or affected by the issue. Certain people are likely to be included where the issue overlaps with their areas of responsibility or expertise. Consider involving people who may have little overlap in responsibility or expertise but have good skills in listening; finding the facts, opinions, feelings and desires; and generating solution(s).

When the issue is defined and individuals involved are identified, a key question to ask is whether the issue is important. Time is valuable and a limited resource. There are more problems or issues in life than a person has time to effectively address. Therefore, it is critical to decide if this is an issue to pursue. If the issue is not important, move on. If the issue is important, prioritize it compared to other important issues and proceed with the Synergy Process. In *Taming the Storm*, the issue was extremely important; it was life threatening.

Once the issue is defined, it is time to understand others. However, the definition of the issue is far from over. In every step along the process, the definition should be quickly reassessed. New information may require partial or total revision of the definition. The intended outcome of the Issue sub-process is to position stakeholders ("Me" and "You") to collect appropriate Information to use in the synergy journey.

Understand You

When Tom realized that he didn't understand what the others were thinking or potential solutions, he was encouraged by Hobbes to use the Understand You process. As Hobbes taught Tom, showing people you truly care causes them to open up and share information. First, Tom willingly listened to John and Simon to understand how they perceived the problem (Pay Attention). He

didn't interrupt them as they provided input because
that tends to direct the conversation and may conceal
the real perceptions of others. As Tom listened, he tried
to categorize the comments into facts, feelings, opinions and desires to ensure he obtained all the Information. Communication is incomplete if any of these elements are missing and it could adversely impact the
quality of the decision. Pay Attention also includes good
eye contact observing body language of the one speaking. Pay Attention also means the listener should control his/her own thought process by minimizing the number of mental trips taken while the other individual is
talking.

After Tom paid attention, he summed up what he
thought he heard John and Simon say (Sum-Up). Sum
up is an executive summary of the important points made
by an individual. The purpose of sum up is to convince
self and others that another individual's point of view is
understood. This step was important to Tom because he
was not used to fishing on the ocean and didn't know if
he really understood John and Simon. The best way to
gain influence with another individual is to first convince the other person that you listened to him/her.

Once the major points were summed up, Tom asked
questions (Ask Questions). The questions were intended
to fill in the gaps where Tom needed to know more about
facts, feelings, opinions or desires. Questions helped Tom
to probe and assess where the group agreed upon points.
Notice, questions are not frequently used during Pay
Attention or Sum Up. The reason for this is that questions tend to direct a conversation toward issues that
are important to Tom, not necessarily John or Simon.
Questions not only tend to direct the conversation, they
tend to stop or hinder thought patterns. Once a question is asked, John may have forgotten or failed to re-

turn to several key points he would have otherwise made during the conversation. During the Pay Attention and Sum-Up steps, it was important for Tom to focus on what was said by John and Simon. When Tom had accomplished Pay Attention, Sum-Up, and Ask Questions, he was able to outline in his own mind the facts, feelings, opinions and desires of both John and Simon. John and Simon were also convinced that Tom understood their point of view increasing Tom's credibility and influence with them. The intended outcome of the Understand You sub-process is to convince the other individuals that their viewpoint is understood.

Understand Me

Once Tom better understood John and Simon, Hobbes nudged Tom toward the Understand Me process. Understand Me or talking to explain your viewpoint is intended to identify the facts, feelings, opinions and desires similar to Understand You.

Tom began by first thinking through or collecting his own thoughts (Think It Through). He structured his points by identifying facts, feelings, opinions and desires. This made it easier for him to present to the others and compare with their points. Once Tom had it clear in his mind, Hobbes encouraged him to share his points with John and Simon.

After Tom shared his Information, it was important for him to summarize the major points (Sum-Up). Similar to the Understand You process, this step gave Tom an executive summary. If John and Simon failed to grasp certain points when Tom first offered his comments, the Sum-Up step should help to cement that point.

Finally, Tom was prepared to answer questions in

order to clarify points that John and Simon may not have understood. Notice that Tom asked for questions. Sometimes it is necessary to do this when others do not come forward with questions (Ask For Questions). The question step allowed Tom to determine if John and Simon understood what he said. By their questions, Tom could understand whether certain points were vague and needed additional information. In Tom's case, the questions flowed without much encouragement. In other situations, it may be necessary to ask for questions and inquire whether points were understood or what reaction they had to specific points. The intended outcome of the Understand Me sub-process is to ensure that other individuals understand your point of view.

Solution(s)

Following the Issue, Understand You and Understand Me steps, the three fishermen were challenged by Hobbes to identify potential Solution(s). Before they could do this, they first had to identify the major information points. Following this, they brainstormed to identify several potential solutions or alternative courses of action to resolve the issue (Develop Options).

In most situations, at least three solutions (mine, yours, ours) are needed to achieve synergy. To sort through several potential solutions, Hobbes offered the fishermen a process. The fishermen were asked to look at each alternative and evaluate the impact of each option (plus and minus) upon "Me" and "You" (Evaluate Impact). "Me" could be an individual, department, organization or group of individuals. "You" are the other people, department, organization or group of individuals involved in the conflict. By adding up the pluses and minuses for each alternative, the leading solution(s) is usually identified as the solution(s) with the highest point value (Pick Best Solution(s)). Once the group confirmed the solution to implement, they had achieved synergy, which led to safety and shore. The intended outcome of the Solution(s) sub-process is to strive for total agreement but settle for no less than consensus. This is the true test of synergy. With agreement in hand, it is now time to implement the Solution(s).

CHAPTER 7

So, What's the Point?

Having read the *Taming the Storm* tale and reviewed the Synergy Model and Synergy Process, it is time to synergize. Only by continued practice can an individual or group become effective synergizer(s). Just like athletes, wind sprints are important. In other words, practice, practice and practice. If not, the key points will be forgotten. The process will become stale.

Right now, identify an issue that is important to you and use the Synergy Process to increase value in an organization or relationship. Consider the issue and think through the facts, feelings, opinions and desires you have related to the issue. Think about the individuals you should include in this process. In other words, identify the people involved in "Me" and "You". You may know some people who are not directly affected by the issue but who would be especially effective participating in the process and add value to the group. Include these people in the dialogue.

When a storm develops, you have choices. You can choose to try and contain the force and manage it. Alternatively, you can choose to avoid the storm. Or, you can choose to use the storm's energy and power and turn it into a strong solution. The best choice is to harness the energy of the storm through SYNERGY.

ABOUT VISIONWORKS, L.L.C.

VisionWorks is dedicated to helping leaders in organizations and individuals in their personal lives to develop and grow through the use of books, workshops, facilitation, personal coaching, consulting and speaking engagements. The foundational belief of VisionWorks is that individuals have an almost unlimited ability to develop and grow. Oftentimes, many individuals are stuck in behaviors where they are dependent on others or independent in their own approach. In a rapidly shrinking world, those who are interdependent in their approach will realize greater rewards, personal satisfaction and harmony.

VisionWorks, through tried and trusted methods, adds long term, sustainable value through focus on:
Leadership Development,
Quality Management,
Organizational Development and
Personal Development.

4119-HORN

Tom Hornsby and Larry Warkoczeski are co-authors of the critically acclaimed book – *New Roles for Leaders: A Step-by-Step Guide to Competitive Advantage*.

If you would like more information about books, materials and/or services from VisionWorks, please contact www.visionworksllc.net

BVG